Original title:
The Mulch Memoirs

Copyright © 2025 Creative Arts Management OÜ
All rights reserved.

Author: Olivia Sterling
ISBN HARDBACK: 978-1-80567-423-8
ISBN PAPERBACK: 978-1-80567-722-2

Resilience in the Rot

Amidst the compost, life does thrive,
Worms throw parties, feel so alive.
A banana peel does a dance so spry,
Who knew old scraps could give it a try?

Sunlight peeks through the garden gate,
While critters debate about their fate.
Even the weeds wear a silly grin,
In this wild chaos, they all fit in.

Layers of Life

In layers thick, we find our spark,
Jokes are hidden—just waiting to embark.
Old food scraps whisper tales in letters,
Unravel joy beneath the fetters.

With every layer, laughter grows,
A cabbage head strikes a pose, it shows.
The carrots giggle, all decked in dirt,
A sassy radish offers an old shirt.

The Hum of Humus

Beneath the surface, whispers collide,
A chorus of critters, in laughter, abide.
Just harmonizing, with roots in the muck,
Plucky little sprouts, unyielding luck.

The earth sings softly, a tuneful delight,
Waltzing in shadows, oh what a sight!
Each crumb a story, be it shabby or grand,
Composters unite with a soil-filled band.

From Ashes to Essence

From ashes to blooms, a tale unfolds,
Charred remains now glisten like gold.
The flames were wild, but don't feel bad,
They sparked new life that's just a tad mad.

With every shoot that reaches high,
Even the ashes can't help but sigh.
In the grand scheme, it's all quite clear,
All beginnings are just reasons to cheer!

Whispers Beneath the Garden Surface

In the dirt, a gossip spree,
Worms share tales, oh so silly!
A carrot dreams of being tall,
While radishes play peek-a-boo with all.

The daisies twist in laughter bright,
As bugs dance round in pure delight.
A beet's bold bragging causes fuss,
Though we all know it's just a plus.

Tales of the Tiller's Touch

A tiller's hum, a joyous tune,
Turning soil beneath the moon.
With every churn, it stirs up cheer,
And plants gossip loud for all to hear.

The seeds hold secrets in their shells,
Awaiting tales the garden tells.
Tomatoes blush, they can't resist,
While peas just laugh, "We're on the list!"

The Circle of Renewal

Nature's dance, a quirky round,
In every shift, new joy is found.
Old leaves fall, then mulch comes in,
What a mess, where to begin?

But out of chaos, sprouts arise,
From soggy tales to azure skies.
Each bloom's a laugh, a chuckle spry,
"Look at me!" they shout, "I'm oh so high!"

From Waste to Wonder

Scraps of dinner, once a chore,
Now lively compost, begging for more.
Old banana peels with a cheerful grin,
Turn into magic, let the fun begin!

With every turn, the laughter grows,
Kitchen heroes, in compost clothes!
From garbage to glory, it's quite a ride,
Join the party, come inside!

Beneath the Leafy Veil

In gardens lush, where secrets hide,
A beetle tripped, but still had pride.
He waltzed with worms in silly glee,
While lettuce chuckled in the spree.

Beneath the leafy veil they danced,
An ant with sass had all entranced.
Bees buzzed jokes, a floral show,
As radishes blushed, 'Oh, please, no!'

Shadows of the Shovel

A shovel once had dreams of flight,
But in the shed, it missed the light.
With every dig, it sang a tune,
Of garden gnomes and flowers' swoon.

It dreamed of skies, of sunny days,
Instead, it shovels dirt in ways.
With patches bright, it found a friend,
As funny tales began to blend.

Dirt Diaries

In journals made of soil and grime,
Worms wrote of love in the springtime.
They scribbled tales of seeds that burst,
And how the beetroot flirted first.

With laughable plots, they penned away,
Of carrots dressed in bright ballet.
A spade got jealous, sulked in need,
While radishes planned their comic deed.

Compost Conversations

In heaps of scraps, where laughter brews,
The citrus peel shared wild old news.
Banana skins cracked a sly joke,
While coffee grounds began to poke.

Potato peel with wisdom said,
'In this great mix, we're all well-fed!'
And earthworms whispered, full of cheer,
'We'll grow a world from what we shear!'

Fertility in the Fog

In the garden, secrets swirl,
Worms in whispers, dance and twirl.
Cabbages giggle under the mist,
While carrots plot an underground tryst.

Morning dew wears a cloak of jest,
As daisies argue, who's the best.
Potatoes boast with muddy pride,
While beet greens lean on each other's side.

Squirrels gossip in leafy shrouds,
"Who planted those?!" they laugh out loud.
Frog serenades echo through the gloom,
While cacti enjoy their silent bloom.

Foggy mornings bring tales anew,
Of leafy romance and laughter too.
In the kingdom of compost and cheer,
Every veggie holds a joke sincere.

Composting Confessions

In the pile, secrets begin to rot,
Banana peels and papers, not what I bought.
Worms don tuxedos, a banquet divine,
But all they eat? My leftover lasagna line.

Splendid scraps whisper tales of woe,
As I confess to a garden of grow.
Eggshells chuckle, "Here comes the rain,
Welcome, dear gardener, to your compost chain."

Coffee grounds moan with caffeinated dread,
"Too much sludge, no more life in the spread!"
While apple cores sing, sweet and refined,
Of better days when they once were aligned.

Still, amidst the rot and peculiar smells,
My garden thrives, and the laughter swells.
In every crumb lies a tale untold,
In laughter and soil, confessions unfold.

Fertile Fantasies

In a patch of dreams where veggies roam,
Tomatoes plot for a taste of foam.
"I'll dress like a berry," they proudly declare,
While cucumbers giggle without a care.

Zucchinis wear capes, ready to soar,
While radishes hide, claiming they're poor.
"What's the secret?!" they all want to know,
As peas roll their eyes, putting on a show.

"Grow faster!" shouts the impatient corn,
While pumpkins boast of what they've worn.
Carrots claim, "I'm the root of it all,"
As peppers rehearse for the next grand ball.

In this garden of whims and desires,
Nature's humor never tires.
From sprout to harvest, the fun doesn't fade,
In fertile fantasies, the jokes are well played.

Paths Through the Perennials

Beneath the blooms, a path appears,
Where daisies tumble, bringing cheers.
Lilies laugh as butterflies dance,
Through this garden, I'll take my chance.

"Hey there, tulips!" I call with glee,
"Have you heard the joke from that wobbly bee?"
As he buzzes on by with a playful sting,
Every flower laughs as if they're king.

Hostas gossip, whispering low,
"Did you see how bright the sunflowers glow?"
And creeping thyme sings in harmonious old,
"Life's a garden—let the stories unfold!"

Through paths where laughter is ever so bright,
Each flower's tale, a joyous delight.
In perennial wisdom, sweet and profound,
The fun in the garden forever is found.

Growth's Gentle Hand

In the garden where the weeds dance,
Earthworms wiggle, they take their chance.
Sprouts shoot up, with a goofy grin,
Whispering secrets on the wind.

Raindrops sing on the leafy tongues,
While bunnies play their silly songs.
Every plant a comedian, it seems,
Telling jokes in their verdant dreams.

The carrots blush, not from the sun,
But from the laughter of everyone.
Tomatoes giggle, ripening bright,
In this wacky garden, all feels right.

A sunflower bows, taking a bow,
Sharing punchlines, who would've know?
In this patch of dirt, so full of glee,
Life's a party, come dance with me!

Soil-Stirred Secrets

Underneath where the roots reside,
Lie tales of mischief, full of pride.
The ants form lines, like a marching band,
Planning their takeovers, oh so grand.

Worms telling tales of soil's delight,
Chuckling softly, all through the night.
Each scoop a treasure, a funny find,
In the realm of dirt, joy's intertwined.

Raccoons peek in, with eyes that shine,
Seeking those secrets, sipping the brine.
They giggle and scurry, such silly sights,
In our animated underworld nights.

A pebble hums a playful tune,
While the moon glows down, a silly balloon.
Nature's comedy in each little patch,
Makes life in the garden a fabulous match!

Rebirth from Remnants

From compost heaps, new lives arise,
With a chuckle and a wink in their eyes.
Potato skins dance, showing their flair,
While broccoli crowns prance in the air.

The old leaves rustle with secrets to share,
Of silly stories, beyond compare.
Carrot tops giggle, waving hello,
In the springtime breeze, they steal the show.

Each sprout a comedian, dressed in green,
Beneath the sun, the silliest scene.
Nature laughs as she plays her part,
Bringing remnant joy, straight from the heart.

With each new bloom, laughter expands,
Life's a circle, as nature commands.
In every corner, fun still remains,
From remnants of yesterday, joy regains!

Tribute to Transience

Petals fall like confetti from the sky,
Each colored moment waves goodbye.
Breezes whisper of time's silly trick,
In this fleeting life, let's learn to stick.

Leaves spin down, the dancers rejoice,
A playful game, without a choice.
Seasons change and the flowers jest,
In their brief lives, they give their best.

Nature's jesters, on a grand parade,
With every bloom, we've all got played.
Beauty too short, but laughter stays,
In memories of these colorful days.

So here's to the short-lived, we cheer loud,
To those bright moments, we're all so proud.
In the garden of life, with laughter we tend,
Each fleeting flower, a funny friend.

Beneath the Garden's Skin

In the earth beneath the sun,
Worms throw parties, oh what fun.
They wiggle, giggle, and dance about,
While roots sip drinks and cheer them out.

Flowers gossip, petals flutter,
'Who's that worm? He's quite a nutter!'
Bees buzz by, a band on tour,
Creating buzz; what's life for, for sure?

Rabbits hop in fancy dress,
Impressing spiders, what a mess!
Each creature's flair a wiggle show,
In this garden, laughter flows.

So grab your spade, don't be shy,
Dig below and see them fly.
For here in dirt, beneath the grin,
Lies a world of joy thick as skin.

The Nutrient Chronicles

Compost piles hold tales untold,
Of veggies bold and greens of gold.
Tomatoes gossip in the shade,
While carrots plot a veggie parade.

Each fruit has secrets, ripe and sweet,
Whispers of growth from root to sheet.
Cabbages clash in leafy brawl,
While peppers pop with humor small.

There's drama here, each seed a star,
In the garden's wild bazaar.
Lettuce laughs, while radishes shove,
It's a comedy of dirt and love.

So join the feast, the tales run deep,
In soil's embrace where roots all creep.
Here's the scoop on who's the best,
In nutrient tales, the roots invest.

Threads of the Underground

Down below in twilight's glow,
Roots are weaving, just like a show.
They stitch their stories, line by line,
In underground threads, they intertwine.

Worms wear hats made of fine clay,
While mushrooms dance the night away.
Rabbits whisper, 'You missed your cue!'
But fungi giggle, 'Not us, you!'

Nuts roll by with a cheeky grin,
Sharing tales of how they skin.
Every inch of soil holds a laugh,
In this mysterious earthy graph.

So take a peek, don't miss the fun,
What's buried deep can't be outdone.
In nature's web, so slyly spun,
The underground revelry's just begun.

Nature's Silent Stories

In the garden, silence speaks,
To leaves that giggle, trunks that sneek.
They tell of squirrels, acorns thrown,
In playfulness of seeds well-grown.

The wind whispers jokes to bees,
Who buzz along with playful ease.
Ivy winks at climbing walls,
While sunlight dances in the calls.

Shadows stretch, as evening falls,
Frogs croak tunes in mellow halls.
Crickets chirp and tap their feet,
Nature's rhythm, soft and sweet.

So listen close, the tales abound,
In every rustle, laugh is found.
Nature's stories, silent yet loud,
In leafy corners, life's unbowed.

Legends of Leaf and Earth

In the garden where the weeds dance,
The gnomes hold a leafy romance.
With hats made of moss, they start to sway,
Telling tales of a bright, sunny day.

The worms in a row sing the soil's praise,
While ants march along in a perfect maze.
Each bug has a story, a laugh, a cheer,
With leaf cups in hand, they toast to good beer.

Frogs croak a tune, as old as the time,
While snails in their shells keep a rhythm and rhyme.
With every soft squish and every small leap,
They giggle at secrets the flowers all keep.

So join in the fun, let the laughter unfurl,
In the land where the oddest of creatures all twirl.
For every leaf tells a tale, true or spun,
In the garden of whimsy, we're never outdone.

Fables from the Forest Floor

Deep in the woods where squirrels play games,
The trees gossip softly, whispering names.
Mice wear tiny hats, sipped acorn chai,
While owls in spectacles watch clouds drift by.

Beneath every root, a secret is found,
As mushrooms play poker with cards underground.
The hedgehogs recite their favorite puns,
Rolling with laughter, under the bright suns.

With branches that creak and trunks that sway,
The forest erupts in a fabulous fray.
Each twig adds a laugh, each leaf a delight,
The critters unite for a whimsical night.

So come take a stroll, let your worries be few,
In the laughter of leaves, you'll find joy anew.
Each fable unfolds, with a chuckle or two,
In the forest's embrace, there's always a zoo.

The Beneath Story

Down in the dirt, where stories entwine,
A family of roots sip on cheap red wine.
With fungi in hats and a party to share,
The tales of the underground dance through the air.

Wiggly worms gossip, swapping old news,
While beetles exchange their most stylish of shoes.
Each stone holds a tale, quite funny and grand,
A comedy club run by the rocks of the land.

The laughs echo softly, through shadows and light,
As roots throw a bash on a magical night.
With every soft giggle, the soil shakes free,
The beneath is a circus, come join in the spree!

So settle in deep, let the roots take the lead,
In the warmth of the earth, you'll find all that you need.
With jokes that are corny and puns that are neat,
The story beneath, is filled with good cheer and sweet.

Earth's Gentle Nurturers

In gardens so bright, where the silly things bloom,
The critters of earth add warmth and some gloom.
With ladybugs laughing in glistening rows,
They tickle the petals, where sunshine still glows.

The bees make a buzz with their sweet little rhymes,
While butterflies chat through the warm summer times.
With glittery wings and laughter in flight,
They dance through the flowers, a curious sight.

Grasshoppers leap from this leaf to that one,
While ants hold a meeting, announcing the fun.
In the soft earthy hum, harmony grows,
With giggles and wiggles, where everyone knows.

So revel in nature's enchanting embrace,
In this merry realm, there's always a space.
For laughter and joy, in green bunches are found,
In the nurturing arms of the earth's gentle ground.

Beneath the Layer of Leaves

Beneath a canopy, creatures play,
A dance of squirrels, hip-hip hooray!
With acorns and nuts, they plot and scheme,
In the snack bar of nature, they live the dream.

A raccoon in shades sips leaf tea,
Whispers of gossip from a bug so free.
The worms write poems on soft, damp ground,
While the ants hold court, all gathered 'round.

Mushrooms wear hats, a sight to behold,
Telling tall tales of treasures untold.
A slug with a smile slides by with flair,
In this leafy world, joy is everywhere.

Each layer a story, a quirky delight,
Life underneath dances, a beautiful sight.
So tiptoe with glee as you wander and roam,
For beneath the leaves, nature feels like home.

Echoes from the Underbrush

From thickets arise the strangest call,
A frog on a lily, dressed for the ball.
With a croak that resembles a tune so sweet,
He serenades insects, a froggy elite.

Beneath the ferns, a hedgehog hides,
Wearing her quills as her comical guides.
A sneaky old fox, with a grin oh so sly,
Plans mischief and mayhem, oh my, oh my!

The bushes are bustling with chatter and cheer,
The raccoons are planning their late-night career.
Legends unfold with each rustling leaf,
As the critters of chaos jump into brief.

So listen intently to what lies beneath,
For echoes of laughter and tales, they bequeath.
In the underbrush world, they're charmingly loud,
A raucous assembly, a whimsical crowd.

Story of the Silent Roots

Deep in the soil where the secrets lie,
The roots weave gossip as the days pass by.
They share jokes in whispers, so sly and discreet,
About trees with wild claims, oh what a feat!

A blossom once bragged it could touch the sky,
While the thorns interjected with an envious sigh.
"I've seen all the places you dream to explore,"
Said the sturdy old oak, with wisdom galore.

The violets giggle, their petals aflame,
While the daisies compete for the garden's best name.
With laughter and jests that nobody sees,
The roots keep a party beneath the trees.

So as seasons change and the petals do fall,
Remember the laughter beneath it all.
For in silent stories, friendships are grown,
In the world of the roots, you're never alone.

Chronicles of Decomposition

Oh, the chatter of decay, a curious song,
Where fungi dance, and the critters belong.
A beetle struts proudly in biodegradable gear,
With each little crunch, there's much to revere.

The leaves take a bow, their time's come to pass,
As the composters rise with a wink and a sass.
"We'll bring back the sparkle, the life you once knew,"
Said the bustling brigade, all wormy and true.

Mold takes the stage with a flourish and grace,
The nutrients mingle in a slow, sweet embrace.
Nature's recycling, a never-finished show,
Where laughter and life continue to flow.

So here's to the process, the funny rebirth,
In the grand cycle of life, we find our worth.
As the earth gives a giggle, we all play a part,
In the chronicles rich, of composting art.

Whispers of Weeds

In gardens green, they sway and dance,
The weeds all whisper, given a chance.
"We're the free spirits, wild and spry!"
"Who needs your rules? Just watch us fly!"

They plot beneath the sun's warm gaze,
While gardeners sweat through tough, long days.
"Chop us down? We'll be back at dawn!"
Laughter lingers, and soon they're gone.

With roots entwined, they share their jokes,
Among the soil and playful folks.
"Why be tame, when chaos is grand?"
They giggle as they take a stand!

So let them giggle, let them grow,
The weeds are wise, and they know how to show.
In every patch and every crack,
They spread their laughter—never look back!

Chronicles of Compost

In a pile so grand, where the scraps convene,
Old veggies tell tales, oh so serene.
"I was a carrot, bright and spry!"
"Now I'm a hero, give me a try!"

Bananas chip in, with raucous delight,
"I was quite slippery, in the moonlight!"
Now I'm the magic under the sun,
Turning into gold, oh what a run!

Eggshells get grumpy, their voices absurd,
"Crack me once more? That's just plain rude!"
Together they giggle, as they decompose,
Turning kitchen scraps into garden prose!

So here's to the pile, where the magic does flow,
In every dark corner, new wonders will grow.
Though some may think it's just trash in a heap,
The stories they whisper are treasure to keep!

Nurturing Narratives

In the garden's heart, where stories bloom,
The plants are authors, dispelling the gloom.
"I grew tall and proud, just wait and see!"
"I'll feed your dreams, just trust in me!"

Petunias gossip, sparking delight,
"Did you hear about Daisy? What a fright!"
While sunflowers chuckle, standing so tall,
"We bask in the sun! Don't we have it all?"

The soil's their canvas, in shades so bright,
Each sprout a chapter, in day and in night.
"In every drop of rain, we find our muse,
It's a lovely tale that we can't refuse!"

So, leave them be, let their stories unfold,
In the garden's embrace, sweet narratives told.
For underneath petals, lies joy to explore,
Each laughter and whisper, leaves us wanting more!

Beneath the Mulch

Under the layers, the secrets lie,
Where the critters laugh and the earthworms sigh.
"We chill in the cool, just vibing away!"
"Who knew a shady life could be such play?"

The ants throw a party, bustling with cheer,
Carrying crumbs, with nothing to fear.
"We're spreading the joy, in our little parade!"
"Underneath plants, magic is made!"

Rabbits peek in, with a giggle and hop,
"What's under the mulch? We can't let it stop!"
With carrots involved, it's a food lover's dream,
Sneaking and snooping; oh, what a scheme!

So tiptoe and whisper, don't wake the ground,
The mysteries below are the best to be found.
In layers of laughter, life carries on,
Under the mulch, where the fun's never gone!

The Journal of Growth

In a garden where veggies play,
Carrots tango, peas in a sway.
Tomatoes gossip, hoarding the light,
While cabbage jokes about a bug's bite.

A turnip claims it's a prized sage,
While weeds laugh from their wild stage.
Chickens scratching, clucking with glee,
Dreaming of egg-cellent company.

Sunshine dances, tickling the leaves,
Nature's antics, no one believes.
Each sprout a joker, each root a clown,
In this garden, no room for a frown.

Silenced by Stone

A rock sat stoic under the sun,
Said, "I'm here, but I have no fun!"
Critters passed by with a laugh and a jest,
While the stone pondered if it was a pest.

One day a worm gave it a poke,
"Lighten up, friend! You're just a big cloak!"
The stone rolled its eyes, tired of the play,
"At least I'm not stuck in a pile all day!"

Then a beetle shared tales from the ground,
"You think you're tough? You're not even round!"
The rock thought hard, it did start to grin,
Maybe not speaking is the ultimate win!

Harmony in Decay

Fungi strut in their colorful coat,
Singing sweet songs on a floating moat.
Pine needles dance to an old, wise beat,
While moss hums softly beneath their feet.

Plenty of laughter in the compost heap,
Where flavors blend and the critters creep.
A snail tells stories of long, winding trails,
While the old banana peel giggles and wails.

In chaos so vibrant, a lesson unfolds,
Life grows from mishaps and tales often told.
Nature's punchlines, rich with appeal,
Proving that laughter is the best fertilizer deal!

Beneath the Flora

Under the leaves where the shadows play,
Critters convene for a light-hearted fray.
A raccoon in shades, oh what a sight!
Jokes about acorns fly through the night.

A grasshopper chirps, "I'm a star on this stage!
But I'm hopping back home, I can't stay in this age!"
The daisies giggle, their petals a-flutter,
As a parade of ants march to a thumping mutter.

Even the flowers join in the laugh,
Swaying and nodding, a whimsical staff.
Under the flora, the world's a delight,
Where humor blossoms and spirits feel light.

A Symphony of Soil Layers

In the realm of roots and worms,
A concert of decay now swarms.
With beetles tapping out their beat,
And fungi dancing 'neath our feet.

The leaves once green, now brown and crushed,
In nature's spa, relax and hush.
Earthworms wiggle, quite the sight,
Composing symphonies at night.

A whisper from each compost heap,
Secrets that the garden keeps.
Layers stacked, a grand parade,
Emerging life, unafraid.

So come and join this earthy tune,
With bug and root beneath the moon.
Resounding laughter through the muck,
In soil's embrace, we find our luck.

Nature's Requiem

Oh, the drama of decomposing leaves,
A tragedy that no one believes.
In the shadows, the critters play,
As nature hosts its grand ballet.

The beetles hum a playful tune,
While maggots swirl like a cartoon.
In this theater of dirt and grime,
The audience nods, enjoying the crime.

A fallen twig, a berry squashed,
In the opera of life, they're all doshed.
With every crunch and every rustle,
Nature's humor is a true bustle.

So raise a glass to the woodland crew,
For laughter sprouts where the green is blue.
In this requiem of earth's delight,
We find our joy in nature's flight.

Memoirs of an Old Mulch Pile

Gather 'round, my friends, and hear,
Of a mulch pile with stories dear.
Once young and fresh, now worn and wise,
With tales that would make you laugh and cry.

It started with leaves, a pile so grand,
Now just a mass that's hard to stand.
"I've seen it all!" the compost says,
While earthworms roll in playful ways.

From pizza crusts to autumn's best,
Life's banquet was a bubbling fest.
"To every gardener's plot I cling,
In dirt I sit, and proudly sing."

So when you pass my weathered mound,
Don't scoff at what you think you've found.
For humor hides in every space,
In dirt and mulch, we find our place.

The Hidden Life of Organic Matter

In the underworld of spoiling snacks,
Lie tales of life, and fun in packs.
Beneath the surface, worms engage,
In the secret life of earth's stage.

Banana peels and lettuce leaves,
Whispering tales that no one believes.
The cabbage groans, the apple grins,
In this dark dance, the fun begins.

"Who knew," asks one old crusty root,
"That we could bust a groove in this suit?"
The laughter echoes through the muck,
As oddities blossom, they feel pure luck.

So, let the compost rise and shine,
For in this chaos, life intertwines.
From unseen depths, let joy emerge,
In organic lore, we find the surge.

When Leaves Turn to Letters

When leaves begin to shiver,
They start to share their tales,
Whispering in breezy quivers,
   Of all the autumn gales.

A maple wrote a sonnet,
An oak composed a play,
While birch lent a sweet sonnet,
   Reflecting on the day.

In crunch beneath our shoes,
They giggle, dance, and shout,
Each color changing hues,
   Like gossip all about.

So if you hear a murmur,
When stepping on the ground,
Just know it's a good rumor,
   In nature's humor found.

Seeds of Reflection

Seeds lie low and ponder,
Beneath the soil so deep,
They dream of fragrant wonders,
While we forget to sleep.

One dreams of being a daisy,
While another hopes for beans,
Yet all agree it's crazy,
To stay stuck in jeans.

They giggle in the dark,
Each tiny seed a cheer,
Imagining a park,
While we just munch on beer.

Their ponderings take flight,
As spring begins to yell,
While we laugh at their plight,
In nature's funny spell.

The Parables of Pollen

Pollen floats like whispers,
A dance of golden dust,
It flirts with the wind's sisters,
A tiny traveler's trust.

Buzzing bees are in on it,
A comic little crew,
They sip, and giggle, and flit,
With sticky feet in view.

"Catch me if you can!" they sing,
As butterflies fly by,
Mixing pollen's joyful bling,
With every fluttered sigh.

There's wisdom in their fun,
Like jokes from nature's shroud,
Each pollen grain a pun,
In laughter they're enshroud.

Underfoot Reveries

Beneath our busy feet,
The soil whispers a dream,
Where earthworms laugh and eat,
In their squiggly regime.

A pebble tells a story,
Of travels far and wide,
While roots share their old glory,
In darkness they confide.

Gravel jokes and chuckles,
As we stomp on by with flair,
Each step that softly buckles,
A serenade in air.

But watch that crunchy ground,
It hums a silly tune,
In secrets all around,
Nature's jesting boon.

The Cycle of Bloom

In gardens where the daisies dance,
The worms throw parties, take a chance.
They wiggle and giggle, without a care,
While squirrels steal sunlight, unaware.

From seeds to sprouts, the stories grow,
The bees hold court, and flowers know.
With petals like hats, they sway and prance,
Creating a ruckus, a floral romance.

The daisies whisper, 'Who's got the best sprout?'
While dandelions shout, 'Check me out!'
Nature's gossip travels far and wide,
In this leafy theater, the bloomers reside.

So join the parade, let laughter bloom,
In the ecosystem's ever-changing room.
Where even the thistles crack a grin,
As the merry cycle of life begins.

Unknown Beneath the Surface

Below the soil, a party brews,
With critters of every shade and hues.
The moles serve snacks, the roots provide drinks,
While gopher DJs spin tunes, no one thinks.

Rabbits tell tales of the grass so golden,
While ants form a line, their wonders beholden.
They trade small secrets, whispers so sweet,
Unknown beneath, where worlds quietly meet.

The earthworms laugh, wearing jackets of dirt,
Poking their heads, they can't help but flirt.
A tangle of laughter, underfoot's delight,
In this hidden realm, all feels just right.

So dig a bit deeper, you might find a crew,
A carnival thriving, where laughter is due.
In shadows and smells, the magic abounds,
Unknown and overlooked, the joy resounds.

Nature's Handwritten History

In every ring of a tree's wide girth,
Lies a funny tale of its time on Earth.
The squirrels muse on years full of fun,
While the branches shake hands with the sun.

The stones tell jokes, with moss as their guide,
They chuckle at roots that twist and slide.
The wildflowers burst, with laughter in bloom,
As bees take the stage, shaking off gloom.

Clouds above are scribbling notes on the breeze,
While butterflies tease the tall swaying trees.
With each passing season, the stories unroll,
Nature's history books, written in soul.

So grab a leaf, join the paper chase,
For nature's history is a comical space.
With whispers of wisdom wrapped in a pun,
Every rustle and giggle, just add to the fun.

Touched by Time

Time tiptoes softly, a sneaky old elf,
Playing hide and seek with the trees on the shelf.
The rocks giggle softly, witnessing all,
As the winds whisper secrets, both big and small.

The blooms roll their eyes at the tick-tock of fate,
While raindrops revive every giggle and trait.
With soil as the canvas, they sketch out their tales,
Of time's playful dance, like a ship with no sails.

The clouds like to prance, shaping stories in air,
While the sun signs autographs, golden and rare.
For life keeps on turning, a riddle we share,
In the theatre of time, there's laughter to spare.

So chuckle with nature as each moment flies,
Touched by time's brush, under wide, open skies.
Join in the merriment, take your place in line,
Where memories flourish, and joy intertwines.

The Life Beneath Our Feet

In shadows deep, where creatures play,
Earthworms dance in the dirt's ballet.
Grubs and bugs in a hidden spree,
A party's brewing, come look and see!

With roots that tickle and leaves that cheer,
The soil holds secrets, both far and near.
Moles dig tunnels, a maze so grand,
Plotting their schemes in our fertile land.

Underfoot giggles and wiggling tails,
Tiny tales of adventurous trails.
A world so silly, where boots can't tread,
A gnome's wild giggle, a mushroom's head!

The ground is alive, with nonsense unheard,
Each wiggle and squirm is utterly absurd.
So next time you ponder, just take a seat,
And laugh at the life beneath your feet!

Vestiges of Verdant Tales

Once were gardens of laugh and cheer,
Now just whispers of what was here.
A cabbage roll's dream gone awry,
Cucumbers plotting to reach for the sky!

Forgotten veggies in rows so neat,
Trying to grow, with a rhythm and beat.
Tomatoes gossip 'neath leafy guise,
While broccoli plots its next big surprise!

The carrots chuckle from their damp hide,
Wishing for sun, with a veggie guide.
Old squash reminisces the days of yore,
When bees would buzz around with a roar.

Though wilted and tired, they still keep score,
Of laughter and love that grew once before.
These tales of greens are but playful dreams,
Woven in dirt and sunshine beams!

The Alchemy of Decay

Leaves fall like feathers, the crunch is divine,
Spiders weave magic, in shadows they shine.
Fungi emerge with a squishy delight,
Turning the remnants of day into night!

A banquet of bugs, oh what a sight,
Feasting on leftovers with sheer appetite.
Mushrooms erupt, with caps all aglow,
In the garden's embrace, they'd put on a show.

The dance of decay brings giggles and grins,
As nature's own show begins where it ends.
Worms wear tuxedos, and critters in peaks,
Swapping fine tales of their humorous feats.

Life in the compost, a banquet of cheer,
Every squish and splash holds treasures quite dear.
So raise up your glass to the rot and the mold,
For in this grand cycle, great stories unfold!

Remnants of the Garden's Heart

In the garden's mess, there lies a joke,
A trowel's tip is bound to provoke.
Potatoes grinning with dirt on their face,
While onions cry—oh, what a disgrace!

Scarecrows stand guard, with straw in their hair,
Warding off pests, pretending to scare.
A radish once snickered, a beet felt sly,
Together they plotted, as friends in the rye.

Compost piles whisper, 'We're just getting old,'
With tales of sweet veggies from stories retold.
Celery chuckled, "I once had great leaves!"
While the tomatoes blushed, "Let's see what he weaves!"

In this wild garden, where laughter is vast,
Old remnants remind us of seasons gone past.
Each joke from the soil, each giggle from roots,
Echoing softly, in old garden boots!

Remnants of Resilience

In gardens where the daisies dance,
A rogue worm gives the soil a chance.
With a wiggle and a little bit of flair,
He burrows deep without a care.

These compost heaps, a treasure trove,
With secrets only fungi know.
Among the scraps of veggies past,
A banquet for the bold is cast.

While sprouts emerge, they sing in glee,
'We owe it all to this debris!'
With chuckles shared by grinning greens,
They frolic there amidst the beans.

So cherish what in life seems bleak,
For in the muck, the roots run deep.
Resilience grows, it won't be shy,
Just take a peek and give a try.

Portrait of a Petal

A lonely petal on a wind-blown wheel,
Struttin' his stuff, oh what a deal!
With colors bright that catch the eye,
He spins around, unsure, but spry.

He took a tumble, a graceful sway,
With all the flair of cabaret!
Waltzing through weeds, he starts to prance,
Made pals with a bug in a bug-eyed dance.

In puddles deep, they splash and flit,
With laughter loud, they just won't quit.
A tiny show in nature's frame,
Each little gust, a wild acclaim.

So here's to petals, all around,
With their silly ways, they astound!
Each twirl and twist an artful jest,
In gardens alive, they are the best.

Elm Shadows and Earth Tones

Underneath that mighty tree,
Where squirrels chatter merrily.
The shadows play their secret games,
And dirt flies up like whipped-up flames.

With earth tones mixed, a canvas grand,
Each footprint tells a tale so bland.
A picnic spread, with crumbs and cheer,
The ants march by, a culinary sphere.

The breeze carries laughter, light and fun,
As blossoms whisper, 'We're not done!'
In every shade, a story's spun,
Join the ruckus, oh come on, run!

For life's too short to sit and frown,
Join in the chuckles going around.
With elm shadows playing on the ground,
You'll find humor waiting to be found.

Eulogy of a Fallen Leaf

A leaf once green, so proud and bold,
Now lies on ground, a story told.
With crumbles crisp and colors bright,
He chuckles softly, 'What a flight!'

Once danced on branches, swirling free,
Now part of soil, a memory.
He mutters low, 'Not all is lost,
In death, there's life, just look at cost!'

A wiggle worm halts to pay his dues,
Says, 'Without you buddy, I'd lose my views!'
As critters gather 'round to gawk,
They swap tall tales, they start to talk.

So here's to leaves that fall with grace,
To lay the ground for next life's race.
With laughter shared in nature's dress,
In every ending, there's newness to bless.

The Poetry of Decay

Leaves fall down with grace,
A symphony of brown,
Worms are dancing in their place,
Fashioning a crown.

Nibbled roots and mushrooms sprout,
Nature's little feast,
Vultures in the garden pout,
Weirdness at the least.

A cabbage with a funky face,
Winks at a withered bean,
Life's a game of slow embrace,
In dirt we find the green!

Yet among the clumps and mounds,
Frogs recite their verse,
In this choir of rotten sounds,
Who's the worst or first?

Hoarding Humus

In the shed, a treasure trove,
Of composted dreams,
Spades of earth I cannot shove,
Amidst my dread regimes.

Trowels marooned on dusty shelves,
Next to pots of clay,
Repurposed from our private elves,
That garden went astray.

Riddled weeds in harmony,
A patch of chaos bright,
Hoarding life like some decree,
In this absurd plight.

Cabbage heads in secret chat,
Gossip and giggles mix,
While squirrels plot to steal my hat,
With little pranks and tricks!

Pas de Deux with the Dandelion

A dance in the wind's embrace,
Golden guests abound,
As dandelions take their place,
In gardens underground.

Spinning round and round we go,
Whirling through the grass,
With every leap we steal the show,
The neighbors stop and pass.

We twirl in pink gumboots bright,
In choreographed delight,
Fleeting moments, pure and light,
As weeds graze on the night.

They laugh when I bow to the ground,
For peanut butter's close,
In this odd, delightful mound,
I toast to what I boast!

Between Tides of Earth

In the soil's shifting sands,
Life whispers laughably,
Mushrooms sprout with goofy bands,
A nature's jubilee.

Old boots resting in repose,
Once proud, now strayed,
Laughter sprouts from where it grows,
In games of cat and played.

Under leaves a gnome peeks through,
Serenading with a wink,
Between the tides, we're never blue,
Just twinkling on the brink.

Dirt-stained hands and muddy shoes,
Shuffling as we cheer,
From our patch, we will not lose,
In this earthbound career!

Rebirth in the Garden's Fold

In the dirt where gnomes have tread,
An old sock and a garden shed.
Worms conspire with shy little birds,
Plotting mischief without any words.

Sunflowers strut with their golden crowns,
While carrots wear their leafy gowns.
The radishes giggle, their roots in a twist,
As bugs do a dance, they can't resist.

Frogs croak tales of the weather's whim,
While daisies gossip about the hymn.
Life in the soil, a comical mess,
With nature's humor, we're all in a dress.

So grab a trowel, let laughter unfold,
In the garden, where joy is retold.
Each spade brings a chuckle, a cheer in the air,
In this patch of green, we're free from all care.

Dialogues with Decomposing Dreams

Mushrooms chat with pride on their thrones,
While old leaves chuckle over hushed tones.
In the compost, secrets swirl round,
With every crumb, new jokes abound.

The wise old snail tells tales of the past,
Of sun showers and mud, oh how they last!
The raccoons laugh at their discarded loot,
While ants march home in a rhythmic pursuit.

A ladybug winks, her spots in dismay,
As clumsy beetles roll and sway.
In the realm of decay, there's joy in the grime,
For every ending, there's a new rhyme.

So lift the veil on this earthy show,
Where laughter and compost together do grow.
In dreams of decay, we find a delight,
As nature's humor keeps shining bright.

Garden Whispers

Beneath butterfly wings, secrets are spun,
The daisies laugh as they bask in the sun.
The carrots prattle with onions nearby,
While ladybugs giggle and softly sigh.

Digging deep, the roots hold a tune,
As weeds play games with the silver moon.
A quick-footed rabbit hops into view,
With a wink and a hop, he's off, not askew.

The sage shares tales, a wise old stone,
While tomatoes blush, feeling quite grown.
In this tangled dance of leaves and the breeze,
Garden whispers giggle, putting minds at ease.

So stop and listen to their sweet chatter,
In the heart of green, where laughter's the matter.
Amidst the chaos, the fun never fades,
In life's little garden, where humor parades.

Echoes of Earth

In the muck and the mire, laughter resides,
As crickets tell jokes while the night slide.
The dew drops dance to the rhythm of night,
In the echoes of earth, there's joy in the fright.

Our seeds have stories, each one a delight,
From the misadventures of squirrels in flight.
The petals pipe up with a murmuring chime,
In the whispers of spring, they have tales sublime.

The robins give concerts, their songs in the air,
While hedgehogs huddle, a curious pair.
Every rustle brings stories of daring,
In the tangled roots, there's plenty of sharing.

So step into soil where laughter's reborn,
In the echoes of earth, each day is adorned.
With humor sprouting and joy like a seed,
This garden of tales is all that we need.

Grounded in Grace

In a garden where worms dance,
Life takes its merry chance.
With shovels and spades we dig,
Making compost, what a gig!

Sunlight kisses leafy greens,
Weeds waltz, bursting at the seams.
Planting seeds, oh what a thrill,
Nature's bounty, what a fill!

With trowels, laughter fills the air,
The cabbage rolls, it does not care.
Hearts are light, marigolds sway,
In this soil, we find our play.

From spouts of beans to sprouting peas,
Life's in layers like a breeze.
With earthy jokes and roots so deep,
In this fun, we joyfully leap!

Tales of Transformation

Once a humble pile of leaves,
Now a feast for the garden thieves.
A tomato sprouted, oh what a sight,
Dressed in red, feeling quite bright.

Worms in tuxedos work with flair,
Breaking down the kitchen's care.
Glorious chaos beneath the ground,
In this dance, pure joy is found.

From scraps to richness, what a change!
In the soil, life feels so strange.
Nothing wasted, all in play,
Nature's humor leads the way.

With chuckles shared among the greens,
And roots entwined in lively scenes.
The tale of growth brings us grins,
In this garden, humor wins!

Speaking with the Soil

Underneath the chatter and clatter,
The soil whispers, oh what's the matter?
"Compost here and worms unite,
Transforming scraps, what pure delight!"

"Why wait for rain when you can laugh?
Dance with the roots, embrace the half!"
The radishes reply with a grin,
"Let's stir the soil, let the fun begin!"

With silly songs sung to the beans,
A chorus of carrots joins in between.
"Dig a little deeper, find the treasure,
Life is sweeter, beyond all measure!"

Each turn of the spade a new story,
The compost pile shares its glory.
In this land of giggles and toil,
We find our joys hidden in soil.

In the Company of Cabbages

Gather round, come one, come all,
The cabbages have started their ball.
With leafy hats and stems so stout,
They twirl and spin, there's no doubt.

Some tell tales of muddy days,
While others giggle in leafy ways.
They dream of being salad-bound,
In this gathering, joy is found.

Radishes join with songs of spice,
Each sharing wisdom, isn't it nice?
Together they grow in laughter's light,
Companions in the moonlit night.

With carrots chuckling 'neath the ground,
And beets blushing, laughter resounds.
In the garden, life's a show,
With cabbage friends, we steal the glow!

Beneath the Bark

In the garden, whispers grow,
Beneath the bark where secrets flow.
A squirrel's stash, a tiny hoard,
While crickets sing, the leaves applaud.

Worms hold court in tunnels deep,
Judging if your veggies leap.
They laugh aloud, with soil so rich,
While ants debate who's the best witch.

Toss in the jokes by the old oak tree,
Why did the beetroot hide? Oh, you'll see!
For when it's boiled, it turns a sweet red,
But laughter's the best thing served instead.

So sprinkle some humor and watch it sprout,
With giggles and chuckles, there's never a drought!
In this strange world, beneath the bark,
Funny little things continually embark.

Symphony of Soil

Listen close, the soil sings,
A quirky tune only nature brings.
With each burrow, and every mound,
A silly symphony tightens around.

The worms hum bass, while beetles tap,
As mushrooms dance with an unexpected flap.
"Hey, did you hear what the radish said?
I'm rootin' for you!" they joyously spread.

A grasshopper leaps, with a jazzy leap,
While daisies sway, losing their sheep.
The compost pile holds a grand soirée,
"Guess what? We're all breaking down today!"

With laughter bubbling beneath the top,
Every critter knows, we'll never stop.
In this town of muck, we forget our toil,
As we all groove in the symphony of soil.

Beneath the Green

Well beneath the leafy sheen,
Lives a laughter machine quite unseen.
A snail slides by, cracking jokes at ease,
"Why don't snails drive? No need for keys!"

The daisies laugh with petals wide,
At turtles who take the slowest ride.
"Did you hear? The weeds threw a bash,
But they just wanted to make a splash!"

Sprinkling sunshine, here we play,
Grasstoppers leap in a wild ballet.
"Why do grasshoppers stay clear of school?
They're afraid of the teacher with a rule!"

So come and join this leafy spree,
In our funny world, where all is free.
Beneath the green, the laughter grows,
In secret spots where joy just flows.

Secrets of the Compost

In a pile, old kitchen dreams,
Where potatoes hide and garlic beams.
"Did you hear the carrot's latest joke?
I'm feeling a bit under the yolk!"

Banana peels peel back a grin,
Telling tales of where they've been.
While coffee grounds brew a chuckle or two,
"Why was the bean late? It went to the loo!"

The pile turns round, a merry old caper,
"Let's all meet under the tall paper!"
For secrets shared in the warming sun,
In our compost, there's endless fun.

So laugh with the layers, rich and vast,
Each scrap a story of the future and past.
In the heart of decay, we find our cheer,
In the secrets of the compost, all is clear.

Worms and Wonder

In dark and damp they wiggle and play,
Worms dance their dance in the soil all day.
With a giggle and squirm, they rise up anew,
In the dirt, they create a grand view!

They munch on scraps without any fuss,
Turning trash into treasure, they're a great plus.
With each little nibble, the garden will grow,
Worms are the stars of the underground show!

Fellow earth critters join in the spree,
All working together in harmony.
A laugh from a leaf and a chuckle from peat,
In this comedy club where all friends meet!

So here's to the worms, the wriggling crew,
They turn life to laughter in every hue.
With wiggles and giggles, they show us the way,
How to find joy in a noisy decay!

The Layered Life

Life's like a cake, all layered and thick,
With bits of surprise in each clever stick.
From compost to sprouts, the journey is grand,
Taste-testing the earth's dirty little hand!

Under the mulch, the world finds its zest,
Creating a mess but it sure is the best.
With a sprinkle of worms and a dash of the sun,
Every odd layer becomes part of the fun!

The garden's a mystery, the plot's full of glee,
Where veggies and critters dance wild and free.
Imagine the laughter beneath all that dirt,
When life is a feast, who cares if it's hurt?

So pile on the mulch, let's stack it up right,
In this layered adventure, we'll twirl with delight.
With nature as stage, every plant gets its cue,
Life's silly orchestra plays on, it's true!

Essence of Decay

In the heart of decay, humor still thrives,
Where fungi and bugs are the stars of our lives.
With a squish and a squelch, they lend us their cheer,
Reminding us often that joy's always near!

Beneath smelly layers, the magic's not lost,
With every old banana, there's joy to exhaust.
Turn that blackened junk into fanciful fun,
Decay's just the start, not the end of the run!

A dance of the beetles, a party of flies,
In the essence of decay, there's laughter that flies.
The compost pile hums, it's a jovial mess,
Where life is reborn, making happiness blessed!

So laugh at the mess and embrace all the gray,
In the heart of decay, we find a new way.
With humor and nature, we'll always convey,
Life's teeming with joy, even dressed in decay!

The Language of Leaves

The leaves start to whisper, a rustling delight,
With stories of sunshine and tales of the night.
They giggle in breezes, have secrets to share,
In their fluttering dance, they don't have a care!

Rustling excitement in colors so bright,
They chatter and chuckle in soft morning light.
A showdown of greens, russets, and golds,
In the language of leaves, there's magic retold!

So here in the forest, where shadows play tricks,
The leaves tell their story with whimsical flicks.
With a swish and a sway, they beckon us near,
To join in their laughter, to share in their cheer!

So when next you wander down nature's grand path,
Listen close to the leaves and their joyous laugh.
In every bright flutter, a universe gleams,
The language of leaves whispers whimsical dreams!

Lessons from the Lawn

Grass grows wild, oh what a sight,
In my yard, it rules the night.
I tried to tame it, what a mess,
Now it's a jungle, I confess!

Weeds sneak in, like little spies,
With their sneaky, clever lies.
I swat them down, they laugh and play,
A garden war, a mad cabaret!

The mower roars, it's such a fright,
Chasing stripes of green and white.
But when it sneezes, oh dear me,
A cloud of dust sets my nose free!

So I sit back with some iced tea,
Watching bugs dance, wild and free.
In this lawn saga, I must admit,
Life's a riot—just a bit!

The Scented Saga

A whiff of blooms on a spring day,
Makes me giggle in a silly way.
I sniff a rose, it pricks my nose,
With thorns like points on my prose!

Lavender whispers, 'Come relax!'
But bees' buzz says I should attack.
I swat and squirm, what a clumsy fight,
As the plants chuckle at my plight!

Once I brewed tea from weird herbs,
Felt like a wizard with mighty verbs.
Tasted like dirt, but what a show!
Next time, I'll just let it grow!

In this fragrant world, oh so bright,
Nature giggles from morning till night.
With scents so funny, I can't resist,
Laughter blooms in every twist!

Beneath the Bramble

Underneath thorns, a secret lies,
A world of bugs, not too shy.
With a cricket's tune and a ladybug's grin,
Who knew such chaos could begin?

Rabbits hop with mischief's flair,
While squirrels plot with crafty care.
A wild dance of nature's pranks,
I laugh and gaze as the bramble ranks!

Beneath the bush, a lost sock waits,
Thinking it's found a new fate.
But wait! It's stuck in thickest thorns,
My laundry day's now filled with scorns!

Yet there's a joy in this wild mess,
Every creature claims their dress.
In the tussle of life, with each little scamp,
Laughter sprouts like a vibrant lamp!

Earth's Embrace

In the garden's warm embrace so wide,
I found a worm that tried to hide.
With wiggly moves and a squishy grin,
I couldn't resist; I let the fun begin!

The rhubarb waves, a leafy cheer,
Every breeze tells the tales we hear.
A rogue potato peeks from below,
"Dig me up! I'm ready to go!"

Ants march in lines, like tiny tanks,
Building cities with no thanks.
I sit and watch, an amused onlooker,
As their hustle makes me feel like a booker!

Beneath the stars, where all seems bold,
This earthy fun never gets old.
With laughter shared from sprout to rain,
Life's a patchwork—so playful, unchained!

Garden Whispers

In the garden, all the plants chat,
They gossip secrets, just like a cat.
The carrots giggle, the peas give a wink,
While the broccoli cheers, 'Come on, let's think!'

The daisies dance to the wind's silly tune,
While the radishes plot a springtime balloon.
Tomatoes roll laughter upon the rich soil,
In their leafy retreat, they plot and they toil.

The herbs all agree on a fragrant parade,
Each one with stories, old and well-played.
Chives tell tales of a chomp from a bug,
Parsley just shrugs, 'They're all just a thug.'

So next time you wander where blossoms abound,
Remember the laughter that can be found.
For in gardens whisper, with humor and cheer,
A symphony of life, if you only can hear.

Beneath the Soil's Embrace

Beneath the surface, the worms play their games,
They twist and they turn with no need for names.
In tunnels they giggle, plotting a prank,
A mud-pie surprise right behind the oak plank!

The roots have a meeting, they're forming a band,
"Let's sing to the rain, make it all grand!"
With a tap and a clap, they all join along,
Roots strumming the soil, a harmonized song.

Little beetles march, they think they're so tough,
But the ants just laugh, "You're not that rough!"
Beneath all the chaos, life swirls with delight,
Funny faces abound, hidden from sight.

So dive in the dirt, embrace the odd scene,
You never know what's hiding, unseen.
Laughter flows freely, where soil meets the sun,
In the underworld jests, life's silly and fun.

Tales from the Compost Heap

In the compost heap, a gathering lies,
Old banana peels share their fruity goodbyes.
While coffee grounds chuckle at yesterday's brews,
They swap all their stories, with laughs and with snooze!

Eggshells recite tales of falling from grace,
"Crack me a joke, I need a new place!"
Potato skins join for the laugh of the year,
'Tangled up roots, it's all just good cheer!'

The leaves tumble down, with a raucous delight,
As they reminisce on a wild autumn night.
"Remember the wind?" they giggle and sigh,
"Gathering round, like seeds we can fly!"

So swing by the heap, where the quirky things lay,
Find humor in trash and you'll brighten your day.
For in every old scrap, a chuckle will bloom,
Life in the compost, it's not just for gloom.

Secrets of the Earth's Blanket

Under the blanket, where the critters play,
Secrets are stirred in the mulch every day.
The beetles exchange rumors, in hushed little tones,
While the worms roll in laughter, creating their thrones.

Sticks and leaves whisper of dances in rain,
They've seen all the antics, the laughter, the pain.
When the winds come a-howlin', they whisper with glee,
"Look at that squirrel, as silly as can be!"

Mice tell their tales of a tussle with cheese,
While the spiders weave webs, oh such expert tease.
In this rich, cozy world, where giggles abound,
Nature's own comedy club is perfectly found.

So wrap yourself tight in this earthy embrace,
With joy all around, it's a magical place.
Each creature a player in a whimsical show,
Under the cover, where laughter will grow.

Tales from the Trowel

In gardens where the daisies dance,
A trowel's tale is full of chance.
It digs and scrapes through earth and mud,
Unraveling tales of worms and crud.

With every scoop, a treasure found,
Potatoes hiding underground.
A gnome looks on, with crooked grin,
He's digging too, or just pretending?

The shovel laughs, the rake does sway,
As garden critters join the play.
Weeds cheer on in vibrant green,
While the tulips strut, if you know what I mean!

So grab your tools, let's start the fun,
For every patch, a story spun.
With soil as ink and roots as quill,
We'll write a saga of chase and thrill.

Roots Unfurled

Deep below where mysteries dwell,
Roots weave stories they just can't tell.
A carrot's dream of being bold,
While radishes' secrets go untold.

A garden party, oh what a sight,
With beetroot blushing, feeling right.
The onions layer on their woes,
While sprouts gossip, and gossip grows.

Underneath the leafy spread,
The whispers buzz as laughter spreads.
'The grass is greener!' one claims loud,
While dandelions puff up proud.

So within the soil, tales are spun,
In every crack, a jokester's pun.
With roots unfurling, laughter thrums,
Join the dance beneath the drums!

Nature's Forgotten Chronicles

In shadowy spots, stories hide,
Where critters prance and mushrooms bide.
A tale of snails who dream in pastel,
While ladybugs gossip, oh can't you tell?

The wise old oak stands tall with pride,
Spinning yarns of the squirrels' ride.
They chased their tails in a whirlwind dance,
While daring ants seized their chance.

Amongst the hedges, a whisper runs,
The hedgehogs tell of long-lost fun.
Each twirl and tumble a playful jest,
In this tapestry where all are blessed.

So open your ears to nature's song,
For in these chronicles, you can't go wrong.
A laughter-filled world, so unique and grand,
Where the plants and critters all take a stand!

Fertile Footnotes

In margins where the veggies grow,
There lies a humor we all know.
Radishes cracking jokes so spry,
While beans and peas just laugh and sigh.

Footnotes scribbled in the dirt,
Of blooms and bugs, and joyful hurt.
The bees write stories with every buzz,
While butterflies float, just because.

Tomatoes blush with rosy pride,
While swirling vines have nothing to hide.
'What about the pumpkins?' they tease,
'Whose dreams are big, but guts are seized!'

In this fertile ground of fun and cheer,
Each footnote blooms, oh let's revere!
With laughter sprouting from every seed,
Join the bountiful, joyful creed!

www.ingramcontent.com/pod-product-compliance
Lightning Source LLC
Chambersburg PA
CBHW051634160426
43209CB00004B/638